HOT DUDES
COLORING BOOK

D. C. Taylor

BERKLEY BOOKS, NEW YORK

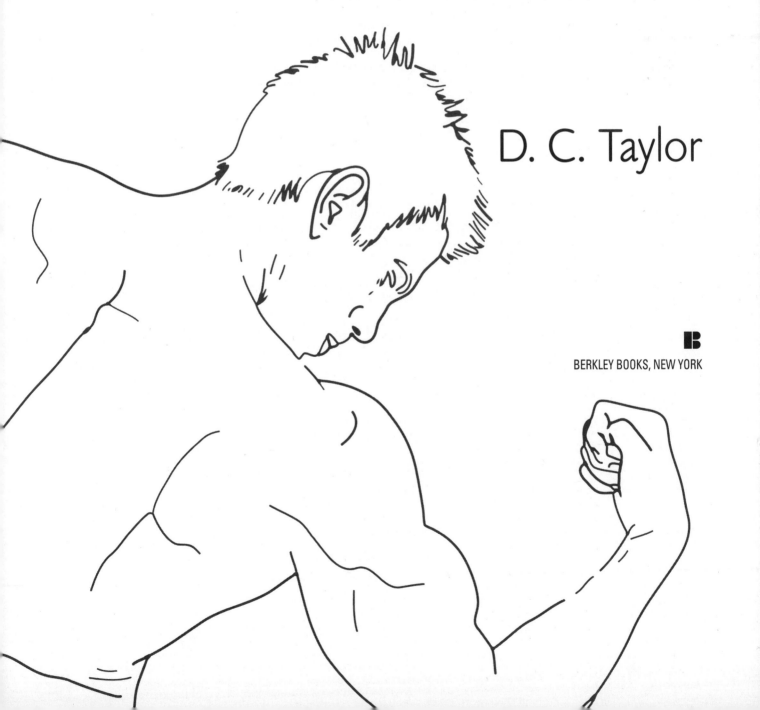

BERKLEY

An imprint of Penguin Random House LLC
375 Hudson Street, New York, New York 10014

This book is an original publication of Penguin Random House LLC.

HOT DUDES COLORING BOOK

Copyright © 2016 by Penguin Random House LLC
Illustrations by Rita Carroll

ISBN: 978-1-101-98724-7

PUBLISHING HISTORY
Berkley trade paperback edition / February 2016

PRINTED IN THE UNITED STATES OF AMERICA

10   9   8   7   6   5   4

Cover design by Rita Carroll.
Interior text design by Kristin del Rosario.

Penguin
Random
House

Thinking about you . . .

Hitching a ride
to your heart.

Wanted:
Hot and Alive

Waiting for the one . . .

Let's spend
the night together.

Brains and brawn

I'd fight off armies
for your heart.

I'm in so deep.

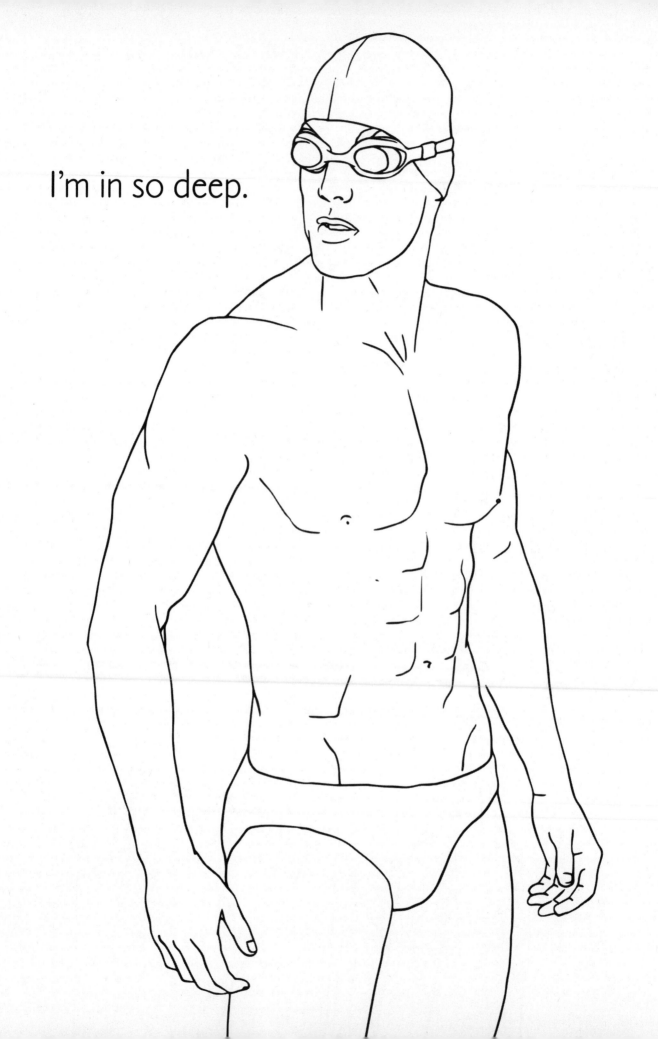

I'm handy
in more ways
than one.

The sky's
the limit.

It's getting
hot in here.

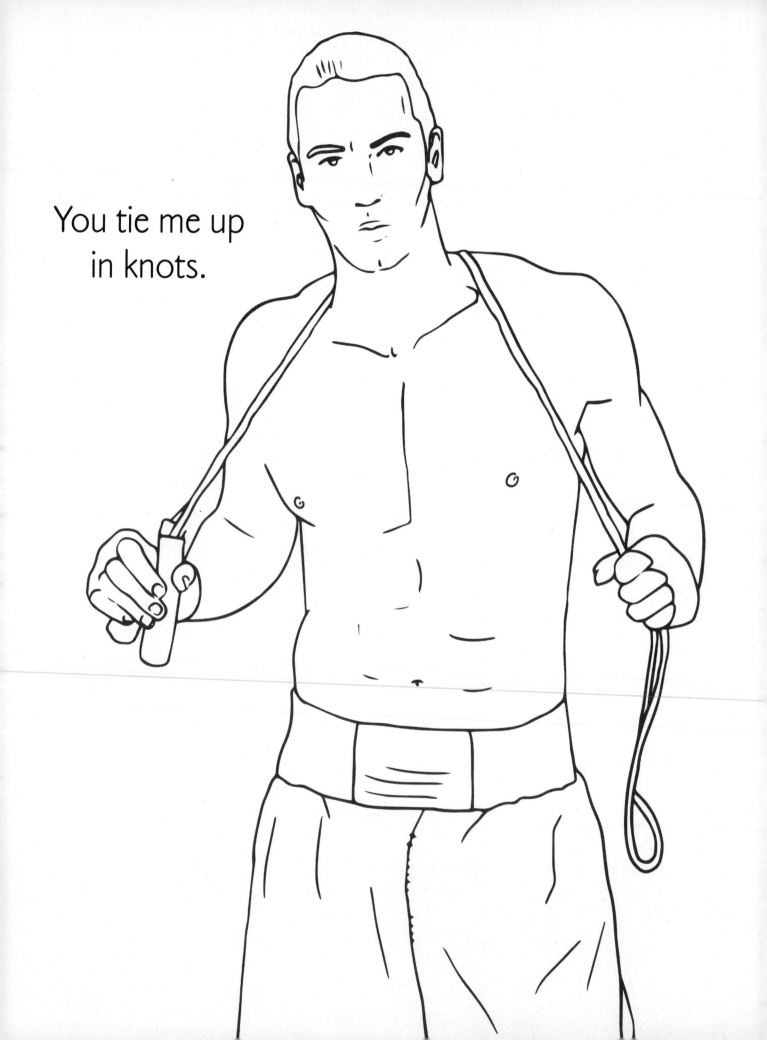

You tie me up
in knots.

Risky business

Easy like Sunday morning.

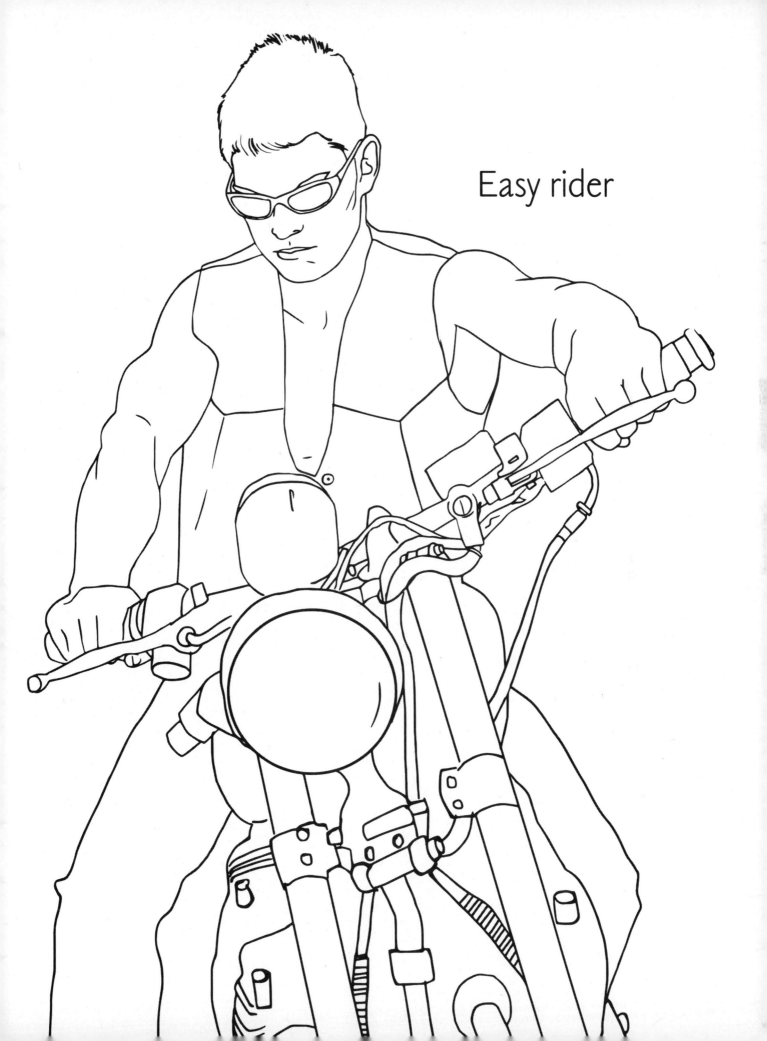

Easy rider

It's hot on the court.

Let's take it
nice and slow.

At your service.

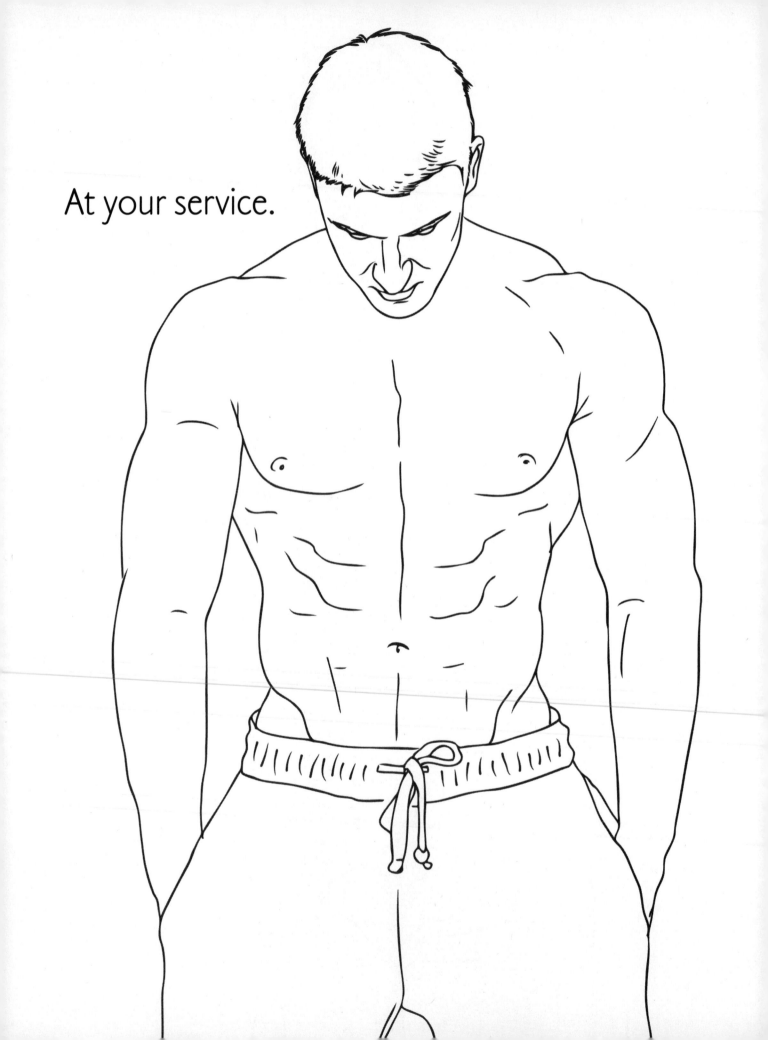

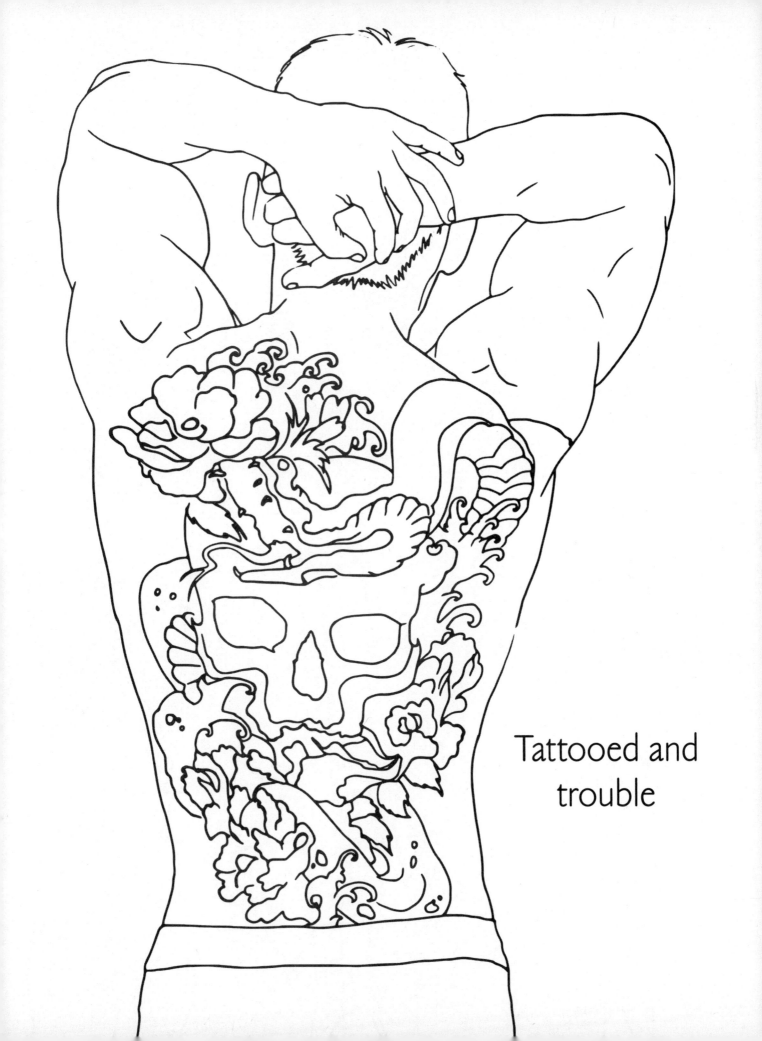

Tattooed and
trouble

A guy who's good with his sword doesn't have to talk much.

I don't mind
getting dirty.

Let's ride off into the sunset together.

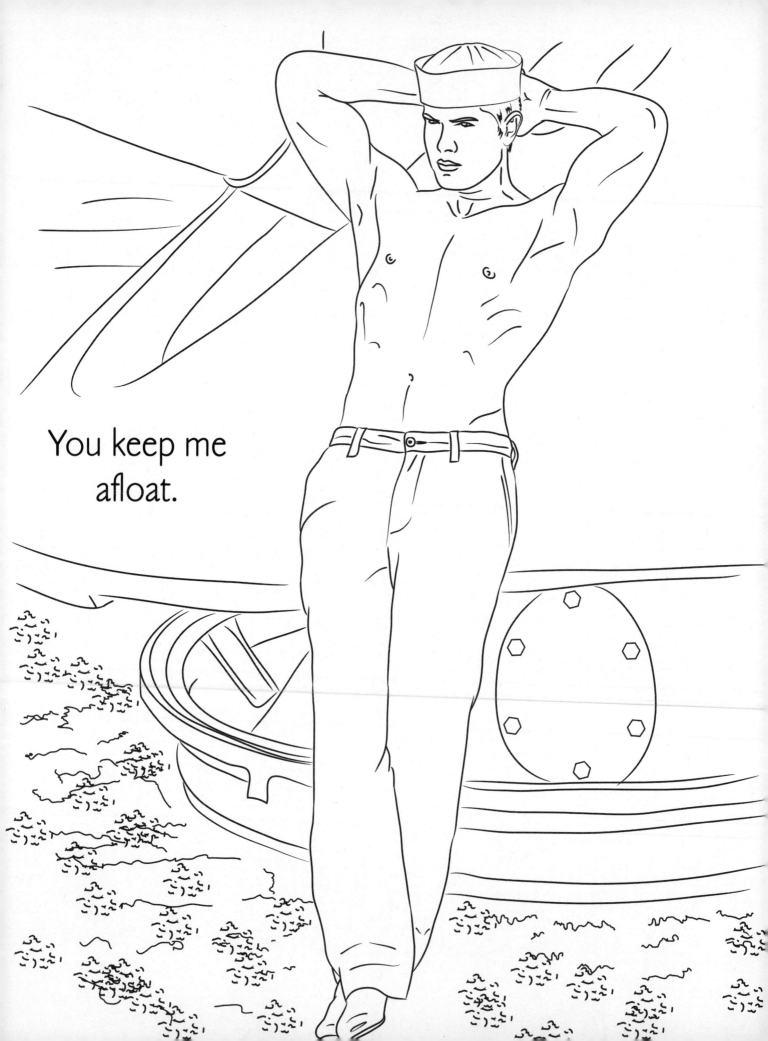

You keep me
afloat.

Too cool
to handle.

Batter up, baby.

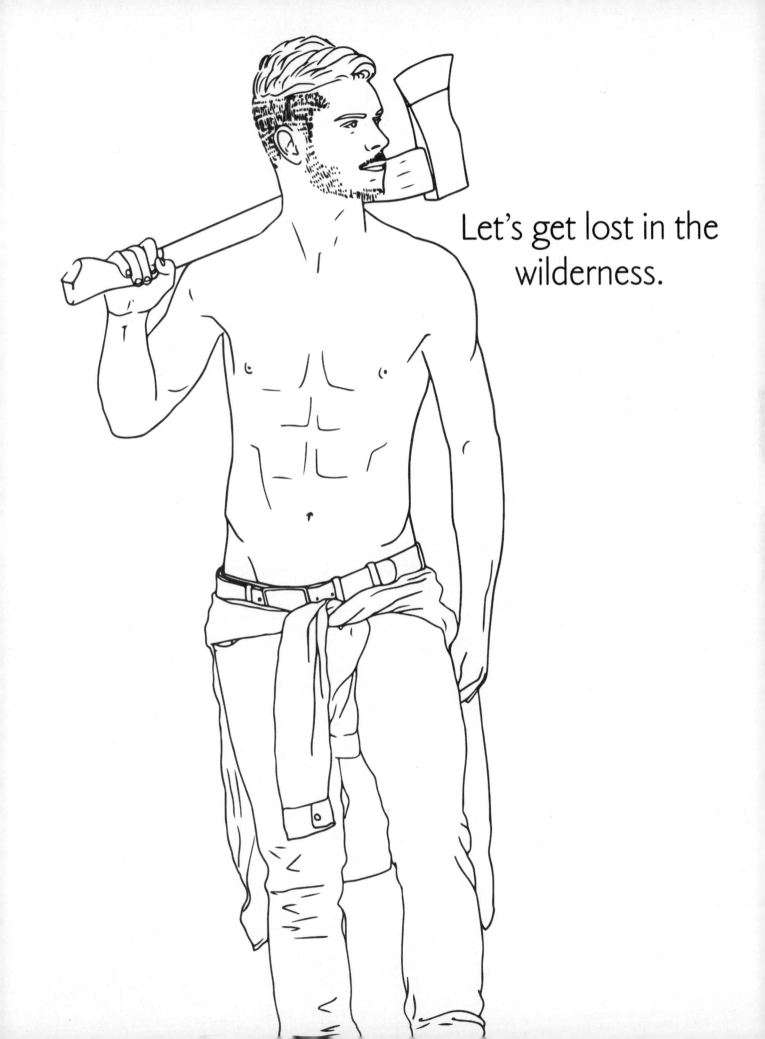

Let's get lost in the wilderness.

We can make
beautiful music
together.

You don't have to hide anything from me.

I swear I'm not
a gold digger, baby.

Let's take it to the mat.

Let's get down
to business.

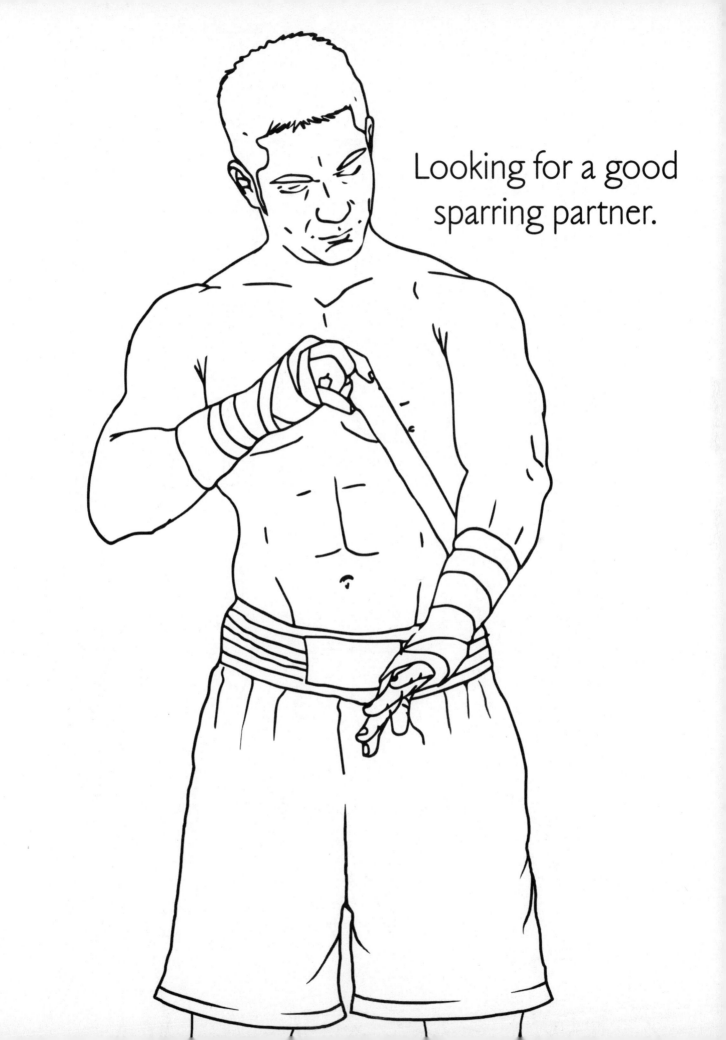

Looking for a good sparring partner.

You're under
house arrest.

Quit playing games
with my heart.

I always score.

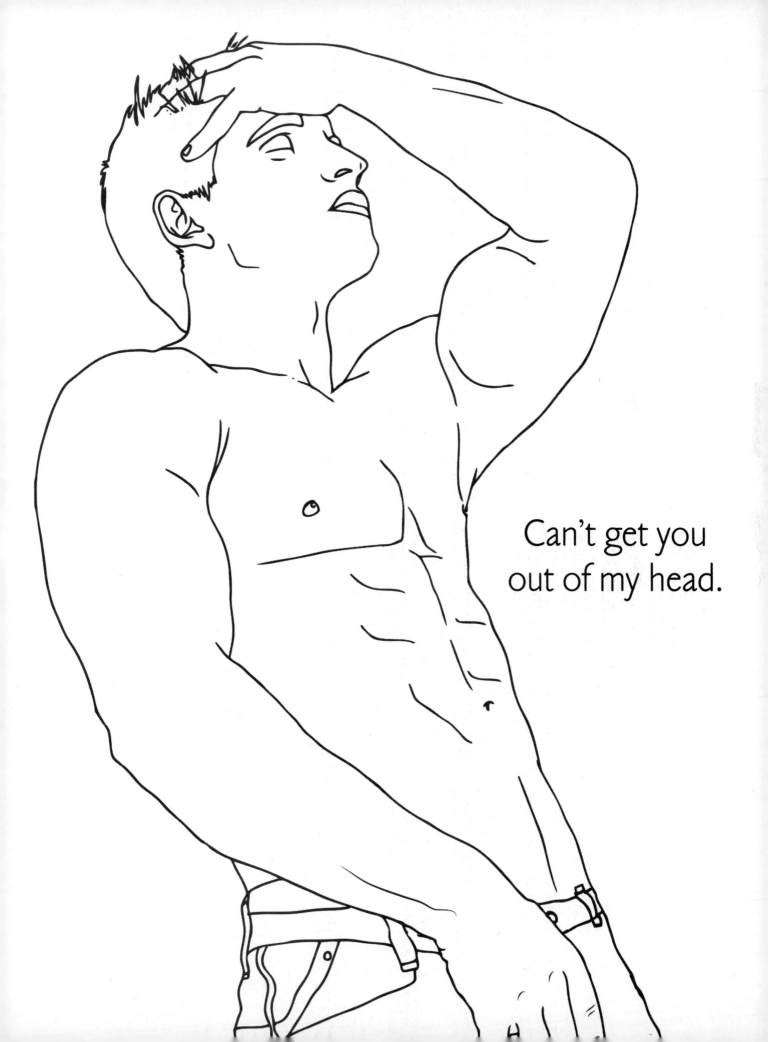

Can't get you
out of my head.

Just me and you
on a hot, deserted island.

Your place or mine?

You've got me
on the ropes.

Are you lonesome tonight?

Let me show you
some moves.

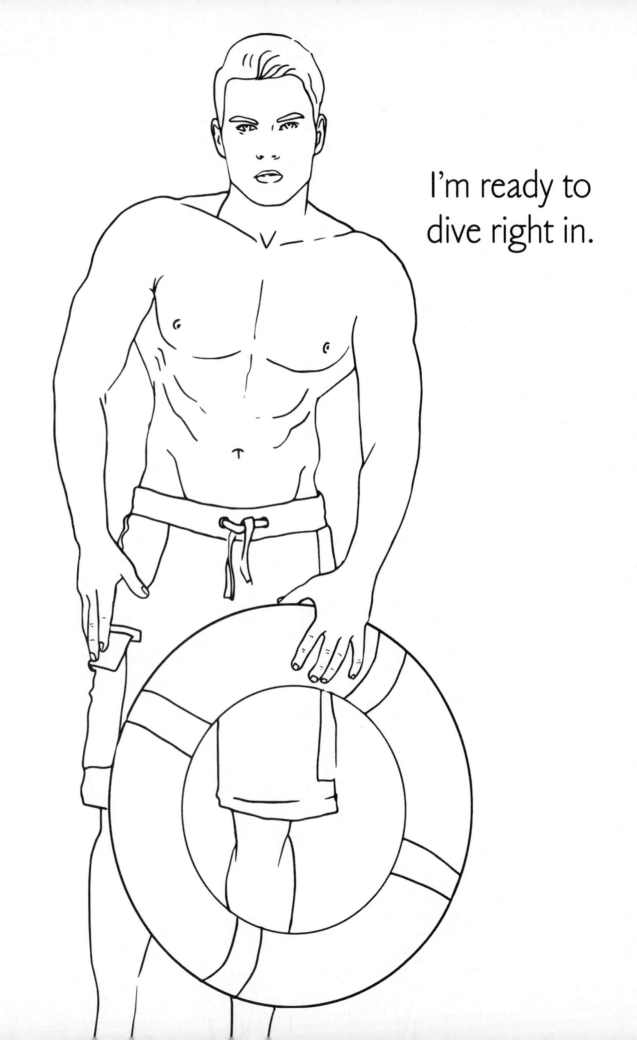

I'm ready to
dive right in.

Looking to score tonight?

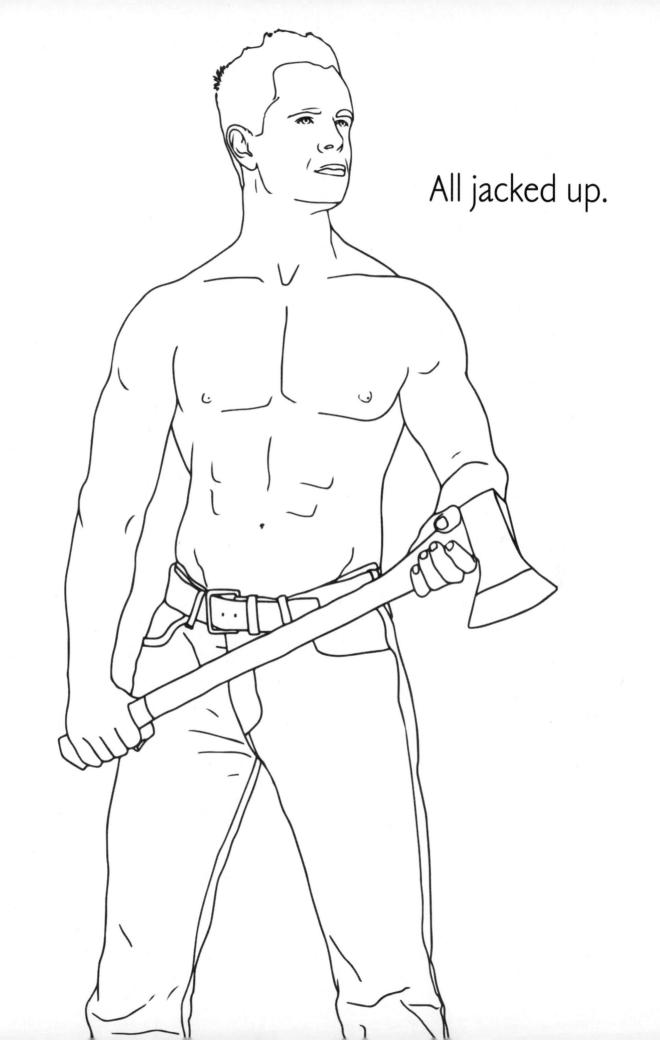

All jacked up.

Take your
best shot—
and score!

Treasure or
pleasure?

I'll put in
overtime
for you.

You knock
me out.

How about some one-on-one?

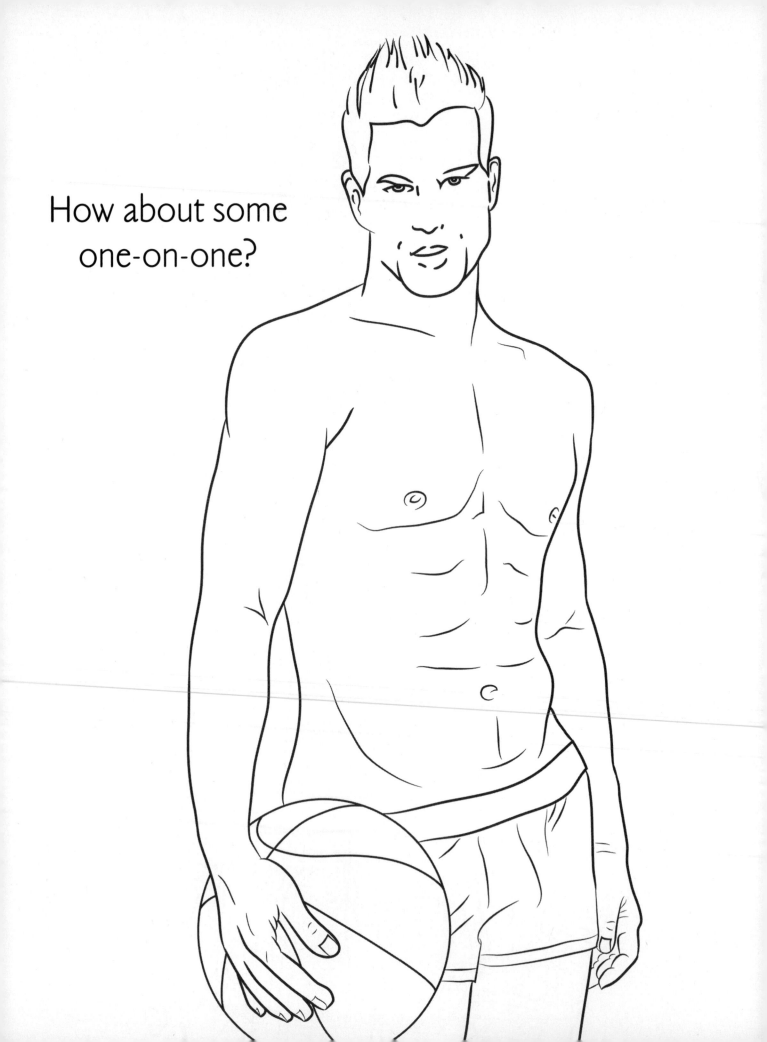

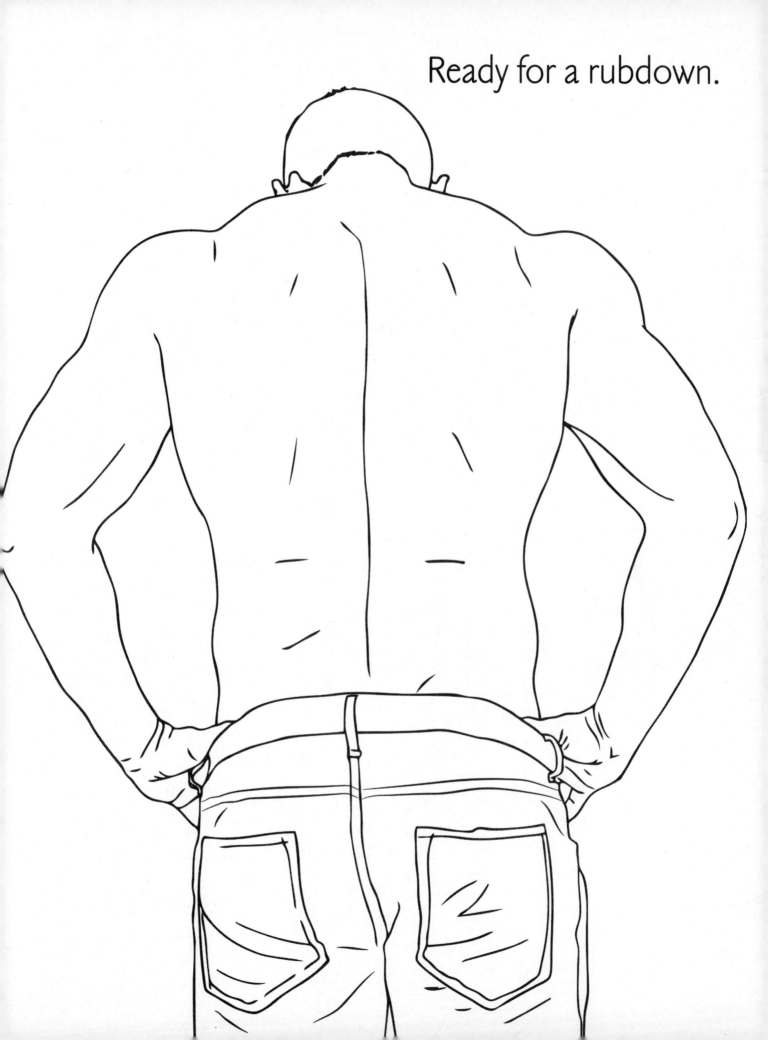

Ready for a rubdown.

Touchdown!

Ready, willing,
and able.

Hard abs,
soft heart.

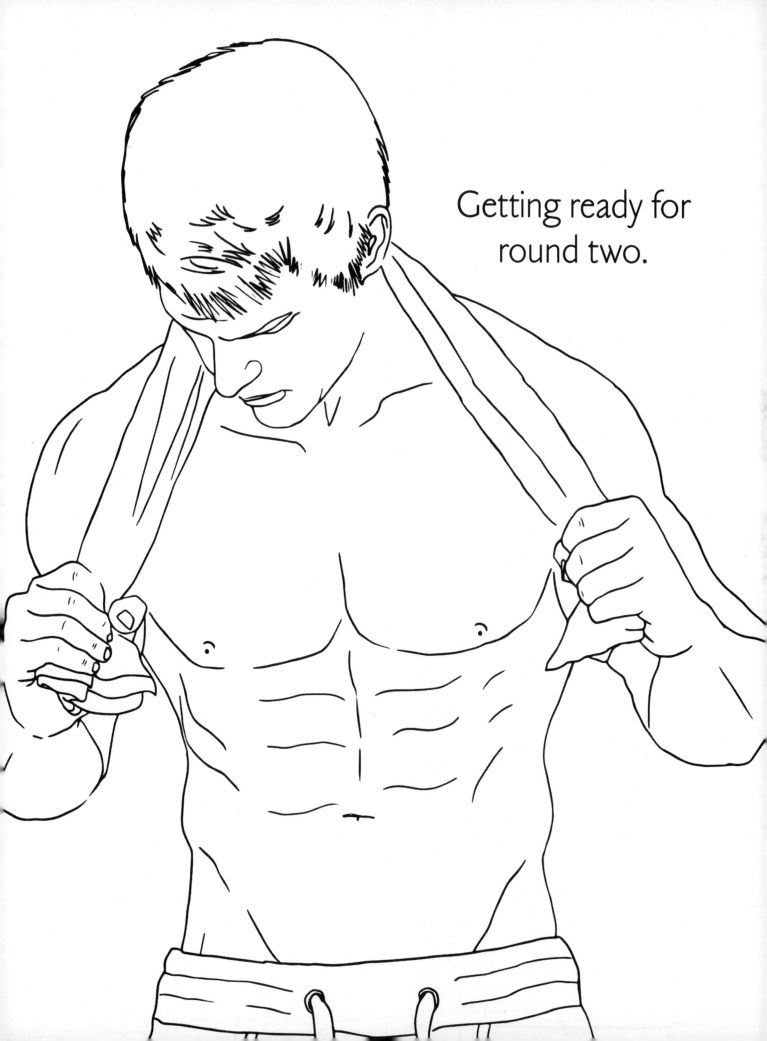

Getting ready for
round two.

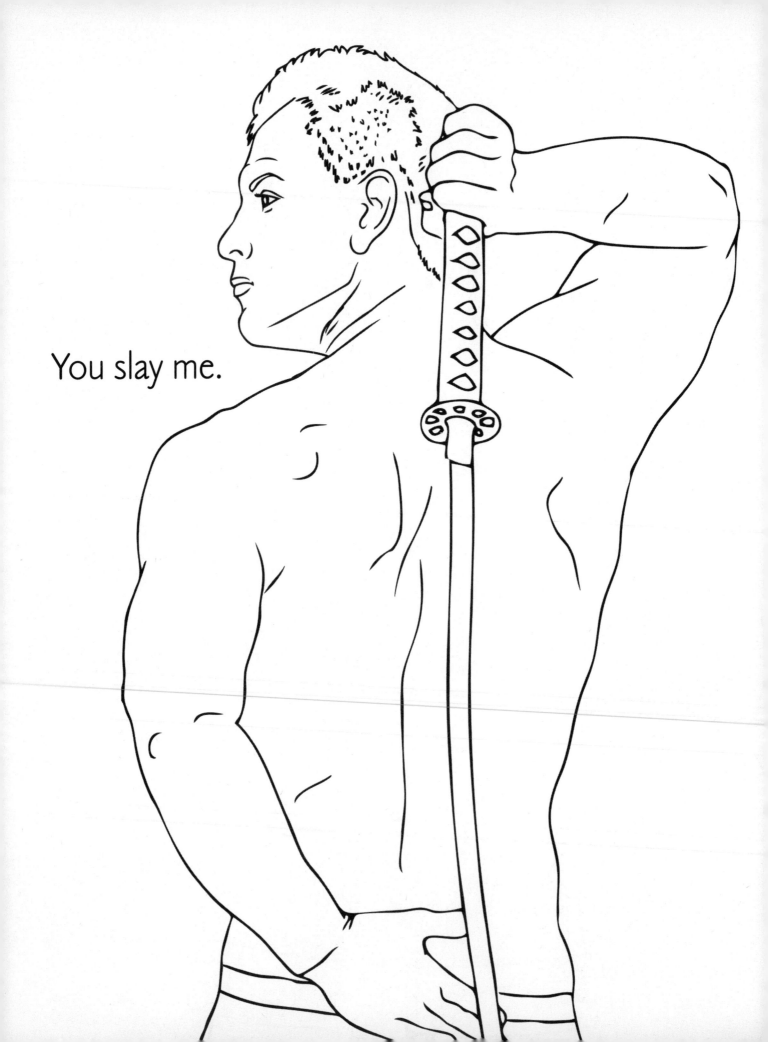

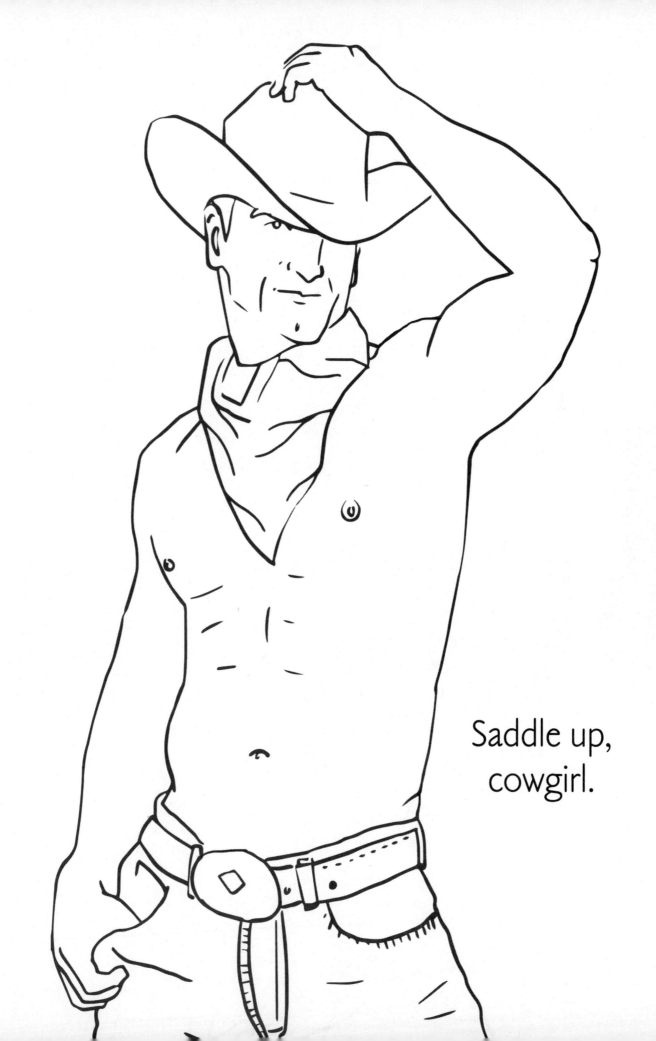

Saddle up,
cowgirl.

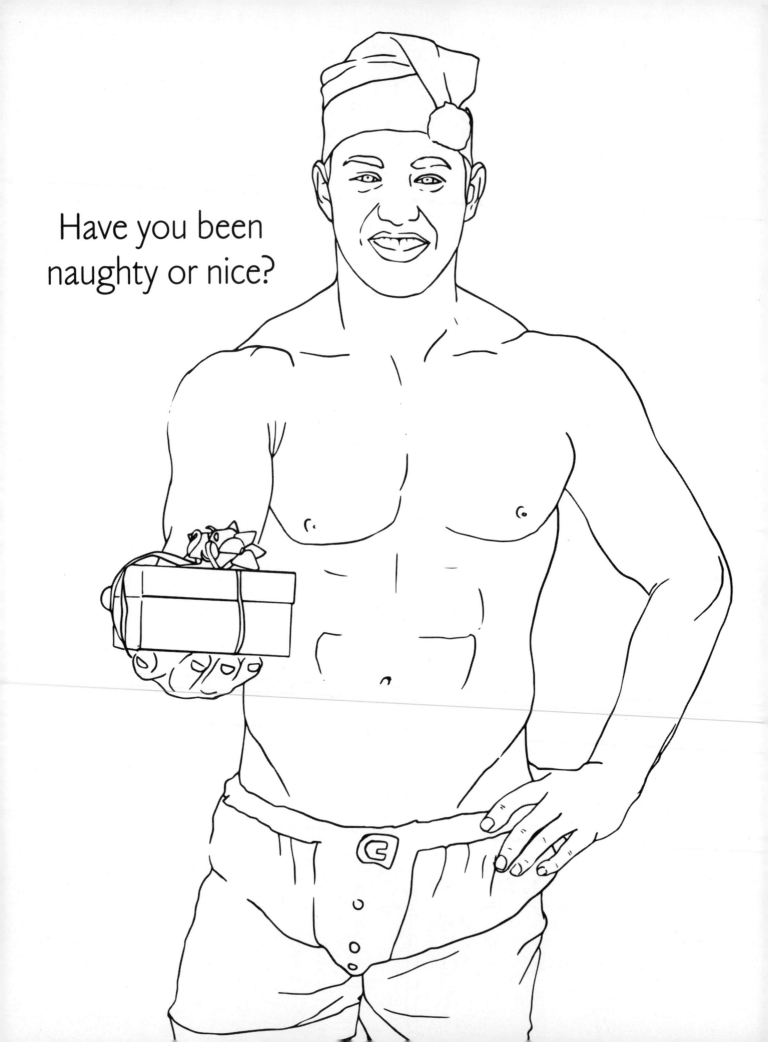

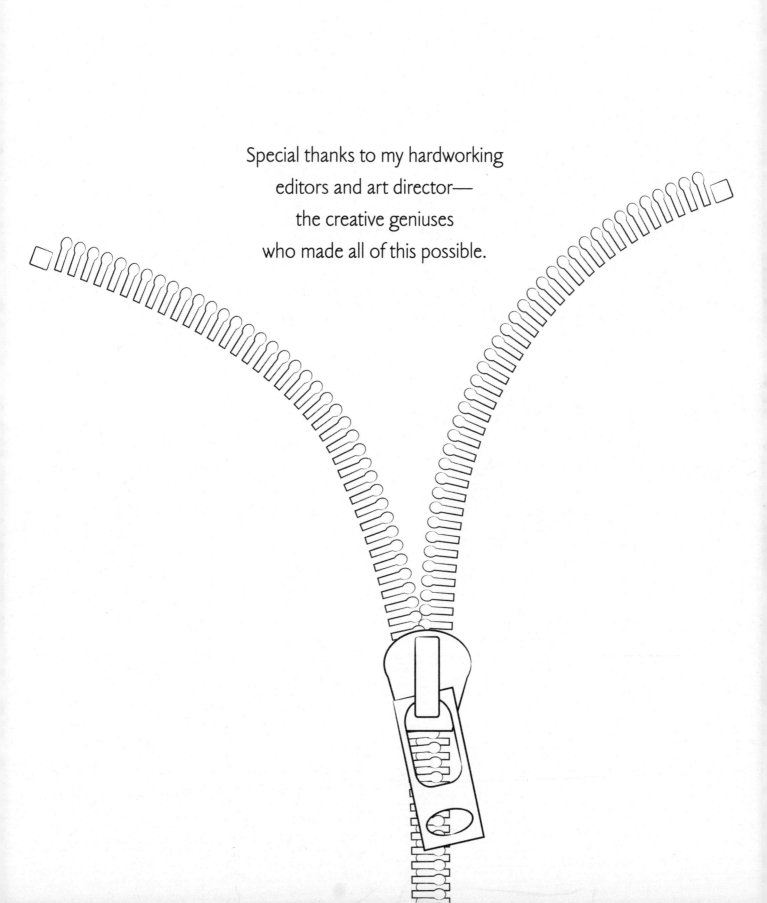

Special thanks to my hardworking
editors and art director—
the creative geniuses
who made all of this possible.